Play Easy Recorder

Compiled by Heather Ramage.
All arrangements by Heather Ramage
unless stated otherwise.
Music engraved by Christopher Hussey.
Cover designed by Ian Butterworth Design.

MIDPOINT PRESS

Volume 1

Away In A Manger

Traditional

Verse 2
The cattle are lowing, the baby awakes,
But little Lord Jesus, no crying he makes.
I love thee, Lord Jesus, look down from the sky,
And stay by my cradle 'til morning is nigh.

My Bonnie Lies Over The Ocean

Traditional

Unchained Melody

Words by Hy Zaret
Music by Alex North

Not too fast ♩. = 72

Oh my love, my dar - ling, I've
hun - gered for your touch a long lone - ly
time. And time goes
by so slow - ly, and time can do so
much. Are you still mine?
I need your love, I

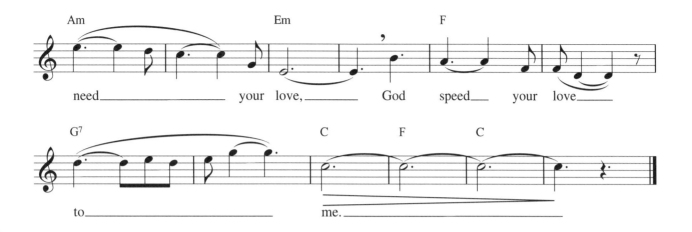

need_____ your love,_____ God speed_____ your love_____ to_____ me.

Amazing Grace

Traditional

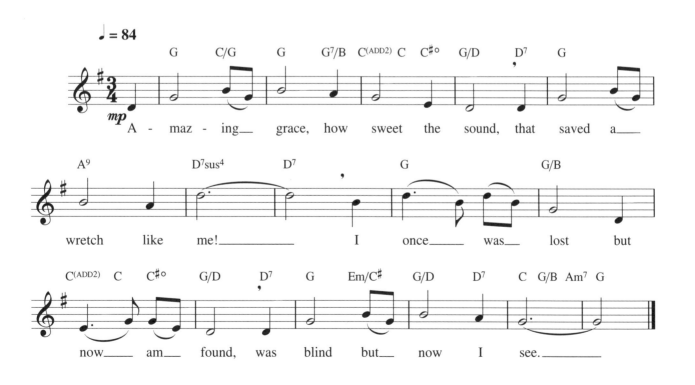

A - maz - ing_____ grace, how sweet the sound, that saved a_____ wretch like me!_____ I once_____ was_____ lost but now_____ am_____ found, was blind but_____ now I see._____

Love Is All Around

Words & Music by Reg Presley
Arranged by Heather Cox

if you real - ly love me, come on and let it show.

You know I love you, I al - ways will,

my mind's made up by the way that I feel. There's

no be - gin - ning there'll be no end, 'cause on my love you

can de - pend.

1.

2.

It's

7

The Blue Danube

By Johann Strauss II

Allegro (tempo di valse)

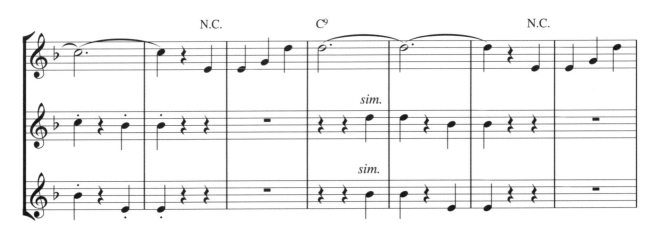

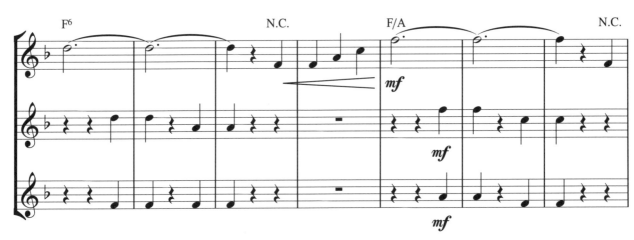

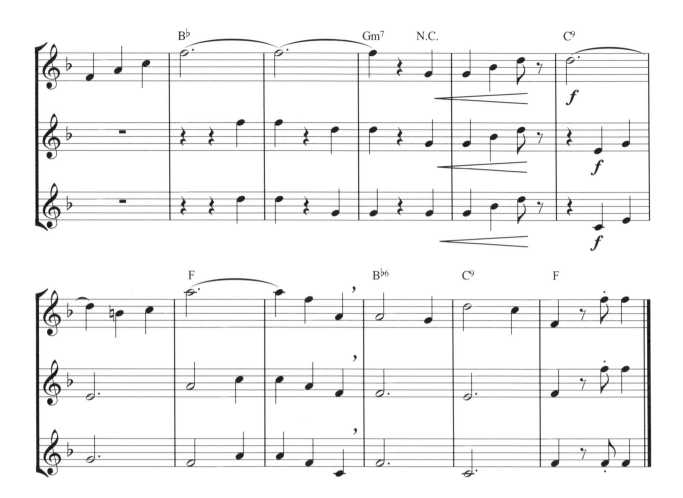

Deep River

Spiritual

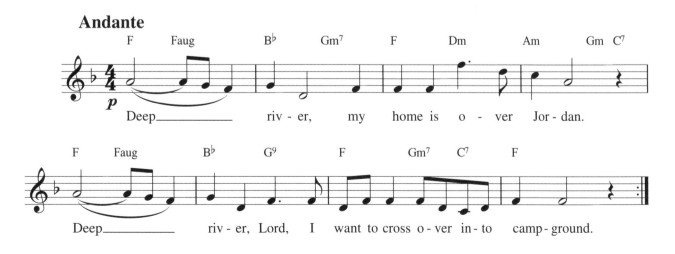

Deep_____ riv - er, my home is o - ver Jor - dan.

Deep_____ riv - er, Lord, I want to cross o - ver in - to camp - ground.

Jingle Bells

By J. S. Pierpont

We're dashing through the snow,
In a one-horse open sleigh,
Across the fields we go;
We're laughing all the way.

The bells on bobtails ring,
They are making spirits bright,
What fun it is to ride and sing
A sleighing song tonight.

Chorus x 2
Oh, jingle bells, jingle bells,
Jingle all the way.
Oh what fun it is to ride
In a one-horse open sleigh!

EastEnders (Theme)

By Leslie Osborne & Simon May

Minuet

(Op.37, No.2)

By James Hook
Arranged by Emma Coulthard

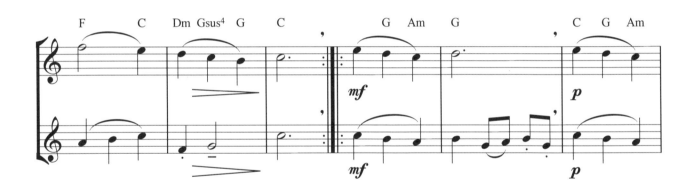

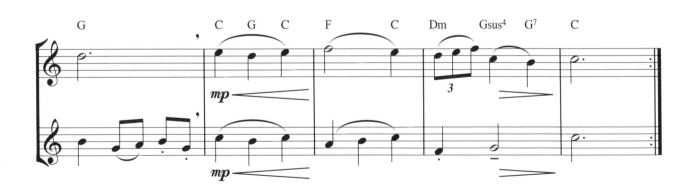

13

Can-Can

By Jacques Offenbach

Con spirito

Jupiter

(from "The Planets")

By Gustav Holst

Andante

Swan Lake (Theme)

By Pyotr Ilyich Tchaikovsky

Moon River

Words by Johnny Mercer
Arranged by Barrie Carson Turner

world. There's such a lot of world to see. _____ We're

cresc.
af - ter the same rain - bow's end. _____

_____ Wait - in' 'round the bend, _____ my Huck - le - ber - ry friend,

1.

dim.
Moon Riv - er _____ and me.

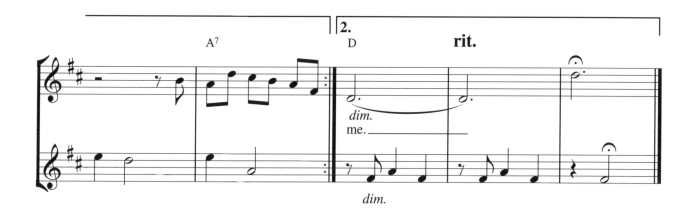

Good King Wenceslas

Traditional

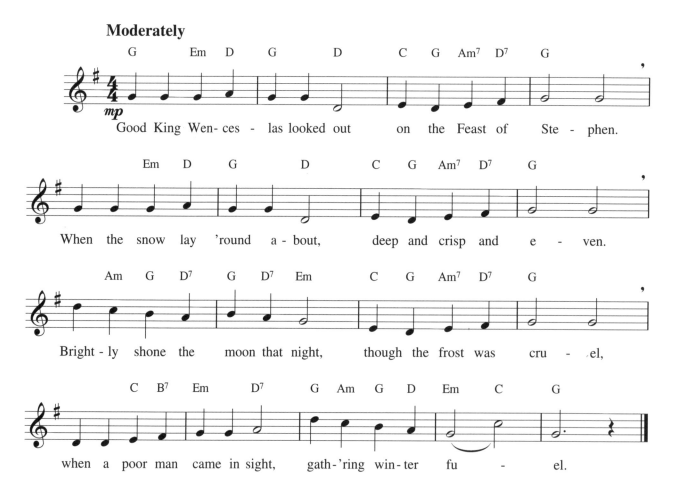

Moderately

Good King Wen- ces - las looked out on the Feast of Ste - phen.

When the snow lay 'round a - bout, deep and crisp and e - ven.

Bright - ly shone the moon that night, though the frost was cru - el,

when a poor man came in sight, gath-'ring win - ter fu - el.

Pelagia's Song

(from "Captain Corelli's Mandolin")

By Stephen Warbeck

Scarborough Fair

Traditional

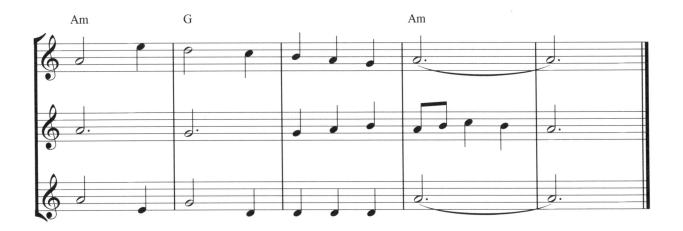

Are you going to Scarborough Fair?
Parsley, sage, rosemary and thyme.
Remember me to one who lives there.
She was once a true love of mine.

Lavender's Blue

Traditional

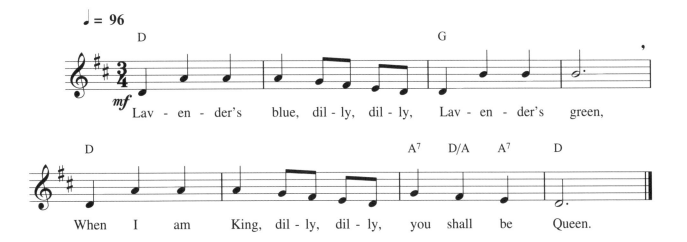

Lav - en - der's blue, dil - ly, dil - ly, Lav - en - der's green,

When I am King, dil - ly, dil - ly, you shall be Queen.

All Love Can Be

Words by Will Jennings
Music by James Horner

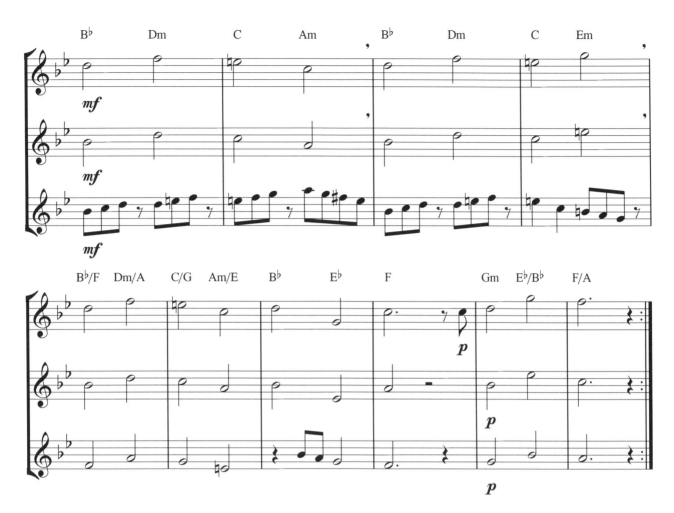

Hot Cross Buns

Traditional

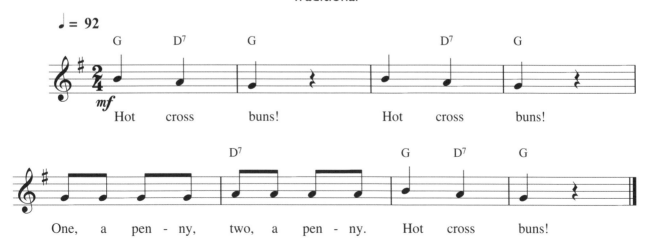

Hot cross buns! Hot cross buns!

One, a pen - ny, two, a pen - ny. Hot cross buns!

Super Trouper

Words & Music by Benny Andersson & Björn Ulvaeus

Moderately

I was sick and tired of ev - 'ry - thing when I called you last night from Glas - gow. All I do is eat and sleep and sing, wish - ing ev - 'ry show was the last show. So i - ma - gine I was glad to hear you're com - ing, sud - den - ly I feel al - right, and it's gon - na be so diff - 'rent when I'm on the stage to - night. To - night the

1. Su - per trou - per lights are gon - na find me, shin - ing like the sun,
2. Su - per trou - per beams are gon - na blind me, but I won't feel blue,

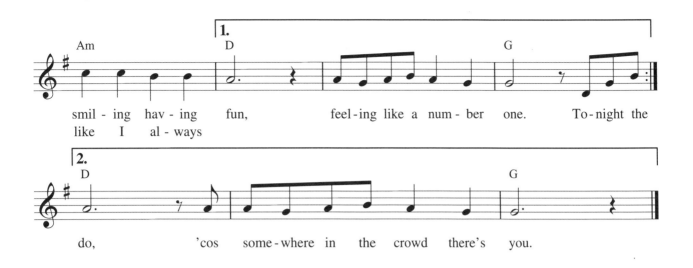

smil-ing hav-ing fun, feel-ing like a num-ber one. To-night the
like I al-ways

do, 'cos some-where in the crowd there's you.

Early One Morning

Traditional

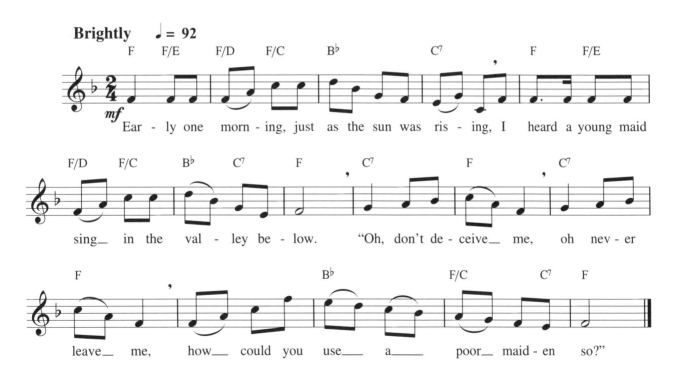

Brightly ♩ = 92

Ear-ly one morn-ing, just as the sun was ris-ing, I heard a young maid

sing___ in the val-ley be-low. "Oh, don't de-ceive___ me, oh nev-er

leave___ me, how___ could you use___ a___ poor___ maid-en so?"

Ob-La-Di, Ob-La-Da

Words & Music by John Lennon & Paul McCartney

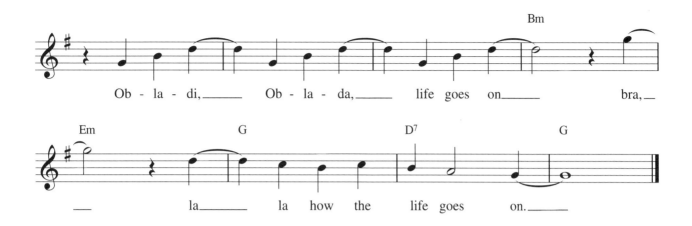

Ob - la - di, _____ Ob - la - da, _____ life goes on _____ bra, _____ la _____ la how the life goes on. _____

God Save The Queen

Traditional

God save our gra-cious Queen; Long live our no-ble Queen; God save the Queen! Send her vic-tor-i-ous, hap-py and glor-i-ous, long to _____ reign _____ o-ver us: God _____ save the Queen!

Can't Smile Without You

Words & Music by Chris Arnold, David Martin & Geoff Morrow

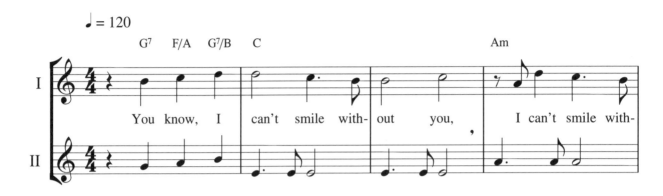

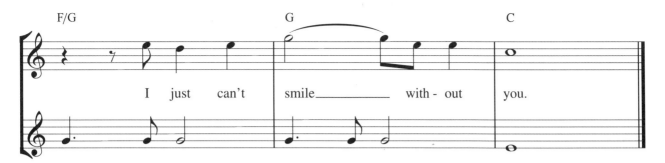

I just can't smile with-out you.

Winter Wonderland

Words by Richard Smith
Music by Felix Bernard

Lazy swing

(sleigh bells can sound throughout)

Sleigh bells ring, are you list-'ning? In the lane snow is

glist-'ning, a beau-ti-ful sight,— we're hap-py to-night,—

walk in' in a win-ter won-der-land. Gone a-way is the blue-bird, here to

stay is a new bird, he sings a love-song as we go a-long,—

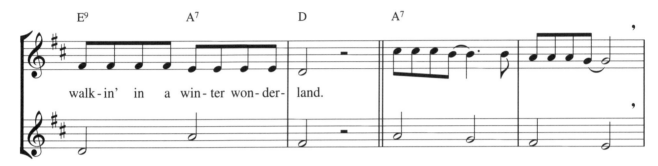

walk-in' in a win-ter won-der-land.

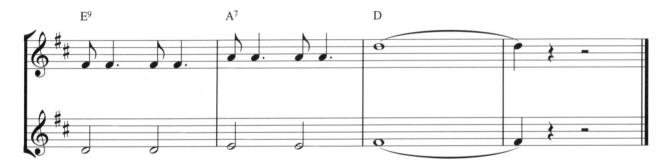

Any Dream Will Do

Music by Andrew Lloyd Webber. Lyrics by Tim Rice
Arranged by Heather Cox and Garth Rickard

With a bounce

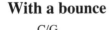

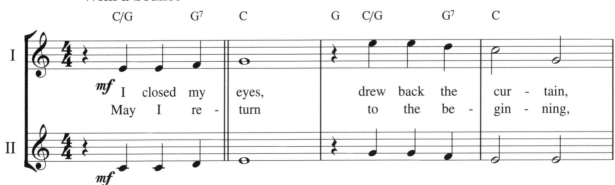

I closed my eyes, drew back the cur-tain,
May I re-turn to the be-gin-ning,

Whole Again

Words & Music by Stuart Kershaw, Andy McCluskey, Bill Padley & Jeremy Godfrey

Soulful ♩ = 80

If you see me walk-ing down the street staring at the sky
If you see me with a - no - ther man laugh-ing and jok-

— and drag-ging my two feet, you just pass me by, it still makes me
-ing do-ing what I can, I won't put you down, 'cos I want you a-

cry, but you can make me whole a - gain.
-round, and you can make me whole a - gain.

Look - in' back on when we first met, I can - not es -

-cape and I can-not for - get. Ba - by you're the one, you still turn me

on, you can make me whole a - gain.

5/04 (51086)